21st Century
Junior Library

# DISABILITIES AND RELATIONSHIPS

**Nicole Evans and Jaxon Sydello**

easterseals

**Understanding Disability**

Published in the United States of America by:

CHERRY LAKE PRESS
2395 South Huron Parkway, Suite 200, Ann Arbor, Michigan 48104
www.cherrylakepress.com

Reading Adviser: Beth Walker Gambro, MS, Ed., Reading Consultant, Yorkville, IL

Photo Credits: © Provided by Easterseals, cover, 1, 5, 7, 11, 18; © Goldsithney/Shutterstock.com, 6;
© Olesia Bilkei/Shutterstock.com, 8, 9; © Denis Kuvaev/Shutterstock.com, 10, 12; © Marco Ciccolella/
Shutterstock.com, 14; © AleTorres/Shutterstock.com, 17

**Cherry Lake Press** is an imprint of Cherry Lake Publishing Group.

Library of Congress Cataloging-in-Publication Data
Names: Evans, Nicole (Nicole Lynn), author. | Sydello, Jaxon, author.
Title: Disabilities and relationships / by Nicole Evans and Jaxon Sydello.
Description: Ann Arbor, Michigan : Cherry Lake Publishing, [2022] | Series: Understanding disability |
    Includes bibliographical references. | Audience: Grades 2-3
Identifiers: LCCN 2022005397 | ISBN 9781668909133 (hardcover) | ISBN 9781668910733 (paperback) |
    ISBN 9781668912324 (ebook) | ISBN 9781668913918 (pdf)
Subjects: LCSH: People with disabilities—Juvenile literature. | Interpersonal relations—Juvenile literature. |
    Disabilities—Juvenile literature.
Classification: LCC HV1568 .E935 2022 | DDC 362.4—dc23/eng/20220211
LC record available at https://lccn.loc.gov/2022005397

Cherry Lake Press would like to acknowledge the work of the Partnership for 21st Century Learning, a Network
of Battelle for Kids. Please visit http://www.battelleforkids.org/networks/p21 for more information.

Printed in the United States of America
Corporate Graphics

Easterseals is enriching education through greater disability equity, inclusion and access. Join us at www.Easterseals.com.

# CONTENTS

# WHAT ARE RELATIONSHIPS?

Relationships are the way two or more people or things are connected to each other. Relationships are formed by how we feel about each other and the activities we do together. We have many types of relationships in our lives. That is exciting! We have relationships with our families, pets, friends, and teachers. People who use **mobility** and **assistive devices** have relationships with their devices.

Relationships are how we are connected to each other.

In every type of relationship, we behave and feel differently. For example, the way you **interact** with your family might be different than the way you interact with your friends. The way someone interacts with mobility or assistive devices might be different from how they interact with their hockey equipment. That is okay! Every relationship is **unique** and special.

Relationships with assistive devices are unique to each person!

**JAXON SAYS:** *I am just like everyone else! I am a big brother, smart student, and fun friend. I am also an excellent sled hockey player and teammate!*

# Think!

Think about all the different relationships you have in your life. How are you connected to other people? How does each relationship make you feel?

# WHY ARE RELATIONSHIPS IMPORTANT?

Healthy, positive, and strong relationships are important because they make us feel good about ourselves. Relationships teach us that we have someone or something to count on and trust during the times when we face **challenges**. If you are having a tough time in school, it is comforting to know that you can talk to trusted people like your family and friends.

# Create!

Write a letter to someone that makes you feel good about yourself. Then give the letter to that person. Show them that you are thankful for this great relationship.

We become better people when we are in healthy, positive, and strong relationships. That's because we learn how to care for other people. It is important to treat people the way we want to be treated.

We all have the desire to love and to be loved. That includes people with disabilities! People with disabilities are caring, loving, and kind people who have relationships just like everyone else.

**JAXON SAYS:** *Just because I have **cerebral palsy** does not mean I should be treated differently. People with disabilities are people too! I treat people the way I want to be treated—like the caring, smart, funny guy I am.*

Healthy relationships are built on trust and respect.

# TYPES OF RELATIONSHIPS

We have many types of relationships throughout our lives. Each relationship is built around how we feel about another person and what activities we do together.

## TEAMMATE RELATIONSHIPS

Teammates, such as those on a sports team, work closely together toward a common goal. A good team is built on trust and **commitment** to each other whether the team wins or loses. Teammates always look out for each other and help each other do better.

**JAXON SAYS:** *I love playing sled hockey! Sled hockey is an **accessible** form of ice hockey for people with disabilities. The best thing about sled hockey is that you do not need your legs to be good at the sport because you sit in a specially designed sled when you play. We even have some players that use **prosthetic** legs! It is fun being on a team because we all get ready together and laugh and joke before the games. When I started sled hockey 5 years ago, I was the youngest on the team. My teammates would always look out for me and would not let anyone bother me while I was on the ice. It feels good to be on a sled hockey team with people like me. We bond over what makes life hard for us, but also get to do something that is so much fun! My relationship with my teammates has made me realize how strong, independent, and loud I can be in life.*

## MOBILITY AND ASSISTIVE DEVICES

At first, it might sound silly to say that we have feelings about objects, but sometimes we do. That is okay! People with disabilities can have relationships with their mobility and assistive devices, too. A mobility or assistive device like a motorized wheelchair or hearing aid helps people with disabilities access the world. Mobility and assistive devices are deeply personal items that are very cool and must always be treated with respect.

**JAXON SAYS:** *I have never named my wheelchair, but if I had to name it, it would be Kevin! I picked Kevin because it is a funny name to me and I like it! I let my peers know that they should not push me or touch my wheelchair unless I say it is okay. If they do not respect my **boundaries**, I do not let them push me.*

# FAMILY RELATIONSHIPS

Family relationships are the emotional connections we have to people we are related to. These include parents, grandparents, siblings, aunts, uncles, and cousins. Family members can be related by birth, marriage, or adoption. You can make anyone else a part of your family, too!

........................................................

**JAXON SAYS:** *My favorite thing to do with my family is get together and have a big meal. My grandma will cook my favorite meals like fried catfish and spaghetti. I love to go camping and hiking with my family, too. When we go hiking, I ride in a special backpack that is designed to carry kids. My mom or dad will carry me on their back so I can experience the hike like everyone else.*

*I also love being an older brother to my sister, Olivia. I get to teach Olivia things about life that I have experienced, and she teaches me things, too! As her big brother, I keep Olivia out of trouble and safe. When we play outside together, I keep an eye on her to make sure she stays in the yard.*

........................................................

# FRIENDSHIPS

Relationships between people who like each other and enjoy each other's company are called friendships. An example of a friend is someone who you enjoy hanging out with and playing games with. You might eat lunch together or play at recess.

**JAXON SAYS:** *My best friend's name is Daniel. We have been friends for 6 years, and it feels like we are family! We met in kindergarten and have been friends ever since. We love to hang out, talk, and laugh. We have sleepovers and play Minecraft and Roblox. I feel comfortable talking about my disability with Daniel. He is the only one that I really express how I feel about having cerebral palsy. Daniel helps me out by carrying my backpack to class in the morning. Sometimes, he helps me out during the school day too—like if there is something difficult for me to open, Daniel will open it for me.*

**JAXON SAYS:** *I also hang out with my friends Gabe and Tej during lunch and at recess. Tej has a disability like I do! This is the first year that I have met another student like me who uses a wheelchair.*

## Make a Guess!

In this chapter, we talked about different types of relationships that you might have in your life. Can you think of any other types of relationships? Write them down and make a list!

# RELATIONSHIPS WITH PHYSICAL THERAPISTS AND AIDES

Sometimes, you may notice your friends or other students with disabilities might have an **aide** with them to help in the classroom and around the school. They might also meet with a **physical therapist** to help them build new skills. These relationships are important because they help people with disabilities develop and grow. People with disabilities may reach **milestones** like exercising, reading, or learning to operate a new wheelchair.

. . . . . . . . . . . . . . . . . . . . . . . . . . . . . . . . . . . . . . . . . . . . . . . . . . . . . . . . . . . . . . . . .

**JAXON SAYS:** *One of my favorite experiences was with my therapist named Barb. She was my therapist from when I was 5 months old to when I was 9 years old. We laughed together so much, and she made therapy fun! I think of Barb as a member of my family.*

*I feel like all my therapists are a part of my family! I know that all my therapists care about all aspects of my life. I know that I can come to them about anything in my life, and they would help me solve the issue or just be an ear to listen to me vent.*

# CREATING GREAT RELATIONSHIPS

Creating and maintaining relationships is important. Being honest, trustworthy, and caring are the keys to a great relationship. Each person must be responsible in a relationship. That is why it is important to treat people the way that you want to be treated. People should also treat you with the same respect and care that you show them.

## Ask Questions!

What do you think is the best way to create a good relationship with your friends or family? Ask your friends or family what is important to them.

Sled hockey is an accessible adaptation of ice hockey designed for players with disabilities. The players are seated on sleds that glide on the ice. The hockey sticks have metal "teeth" that grip the ice. Players use the special sticks to move their sleds and hit the puck.

Did you know that there are a ton of sports that are adapted for people with disabilities? People with disabilities also compete for medals at the Paralympic Games. Check out all the cool adaptive sports at www.paralympic.org.

# GLOSSARY

**accessible (ik-SEH-suh-buhl)** easy to get to or to participate in

**aide (AYD)** an assistant who helps a person with a disability

**assistive devices (uh-SIH-stiv dih-VYE-sez)** objects that can help disabled people navigate their environment, such as grab bars, wheelchairs, lifts, or accessible gaming controllers

**boundaries (BOWN-duh-reez)** limits to an activity or a behavior

**cerebral palsy (suh-REE-bruhl PAHL-zee)** a type of disability that can affect your ability to move, walk, or speak

**challenges (CHAH-luhn-jez)** an interesting or difficult problem or task

**commitment (kuh-MITT-muhnt)** pledge or obligation to fulfill an act or function

**interact (in-tuhr-AKT)** to respond to others in a social situation or have an effect on someone or something

**milestones (MYE-uhl-stohns)** important events or turning points in a person's life

**mobility devices (moh-BIH-luh-tee dih-VYE-sez)** equipment designed to help people with disabilities move, including wheelchairs, walkers, canes, and crutches

**physical therapist (FIH-zih-kuhl THEHR-uh-pist)** trained professional who helps a person with a disability improve movement or manage pain

**prosthetic (PRUHS-theh-tik)** an artificial limb

**unique (yoo-NEEK)** the only one of its type

# FIND OUT MORE

## Books

Burcaw, Shane. *Not So Different: What You Really Want to Ask about Having a Disability.* New York, NY: Roaring Brook Press, 2017.

Burnell, Cerrie. *I Am Not a Label: 34 Disabled Artists, Thinkers, Athletes and Activists from Past and Present.* London, UK: Wide Eyed Editions, 2020.

## Websites

### Get Involved with Easterseals
https://www.easterseals.com/get-involved
Learn about the different ways you can get involved in increasing opportunities for people with disabilities, from advocacy to volunteering.

### YouTube—What Does it Feel Like to be Disabled?
https://youtu.be/TTYI35ldRWU
Listen to Shane Burcaw talk about what it's like to have a disability and why it's not a bad thing.

# INDEX

# ABOUT THE AUTHORS

**Nicole Evans** is an actress, writer, and disability rights and inclusion activist. Born with osteogenesis imperfecta, Nicole is a full-time wheelchair user. She enjoys helping children with disabilities explore their identity and realize their full potential. Nicole lives in Los Angeles, California.

**Jaxon Sydello** is an 11-year-old student, brother, hockey player, and lover of all fun things! He enjoys playing video games and just hanging out with his friends and family. Jax was born with quadriplegic spastic cerebral palsy. Jax mostly uses a manual wheelchair to get around, but he will utilize a reverse walker for short distances. Jax lives in Downers Grove, Illinois, with his mom, dad, and sister.